Coloring For Life

Not So Sweary

A "PG" Collection of Less Than Vulgar Curse Words and Phrases

Hand Drawn Adult Coloring Book Illustrations by Maria Goncalves and Will Williams

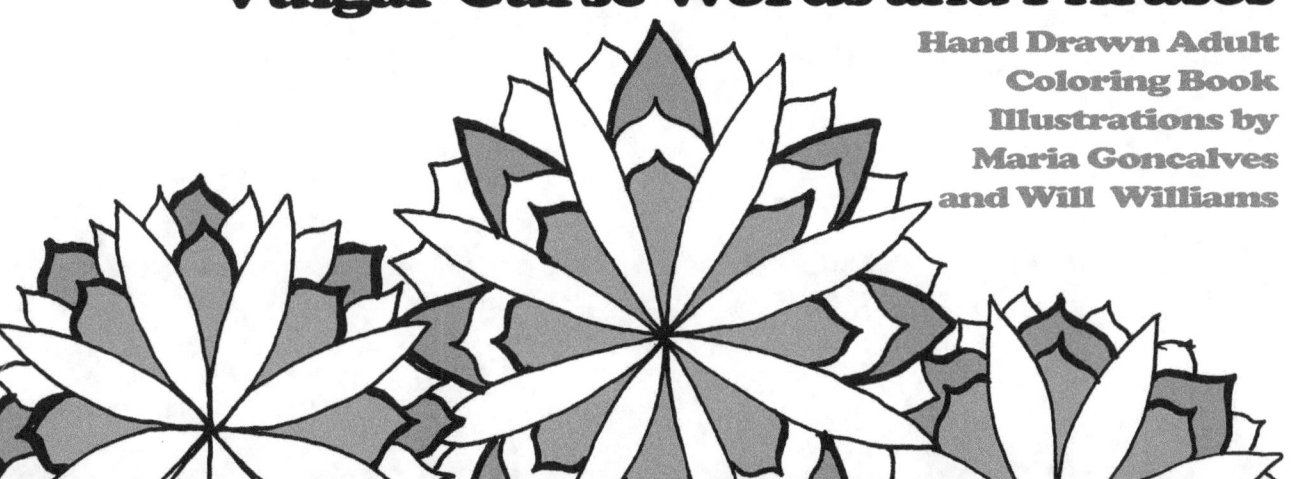

Illustrations by Maria Goncalves and Will Williams
Layout and Design by Bill Clanton

ISBN: 978-0-9974996-5-0

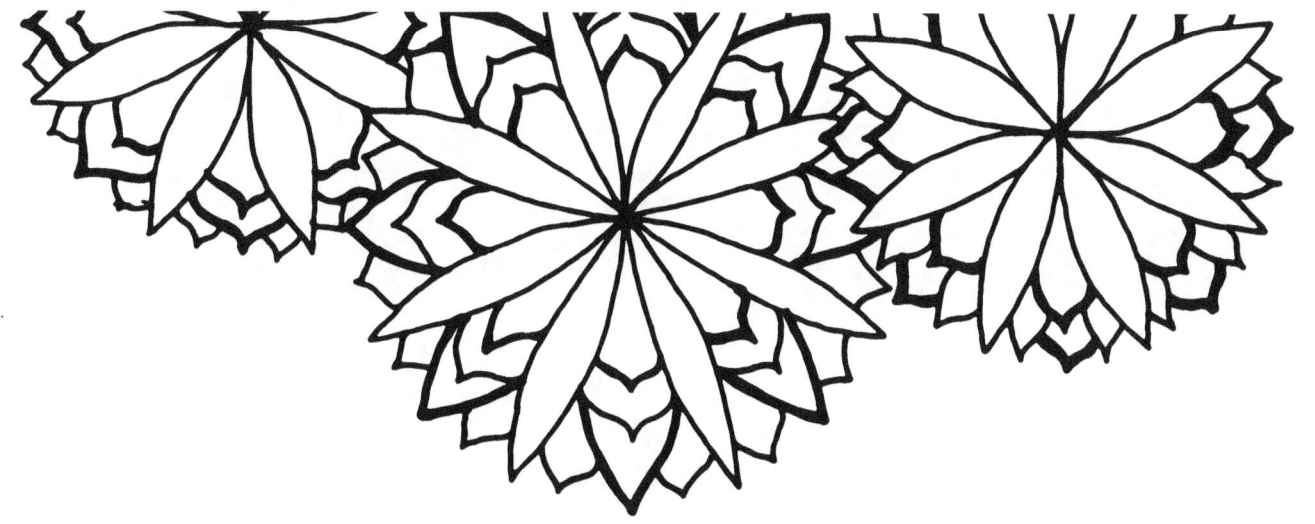

Introduction

We've all had those moments where a full force vulgar curse word is necessary, yet found to be socially unacceptable. So here is an adult coloring book for those times when an alternative curse word is needed. In this book find fun pages to color that will say what needs to be said, but with a purely "PG" rating. So pour yourself a glass of Sugar Honey Iced Tea and Shut Your Pie Hole because this book needs to be colored.

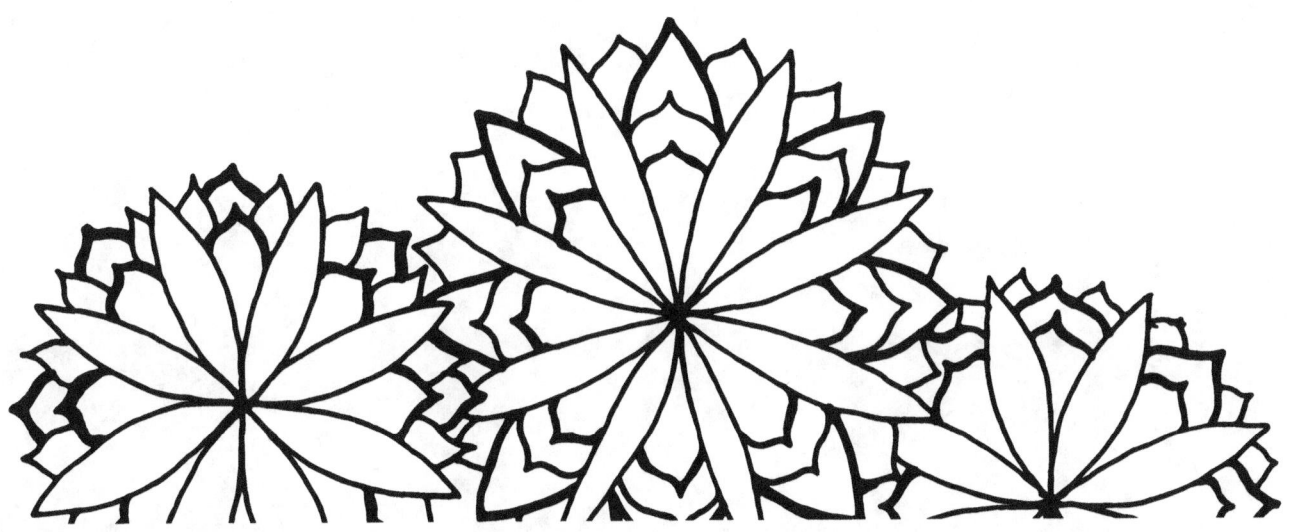

Shut the
Front
Door

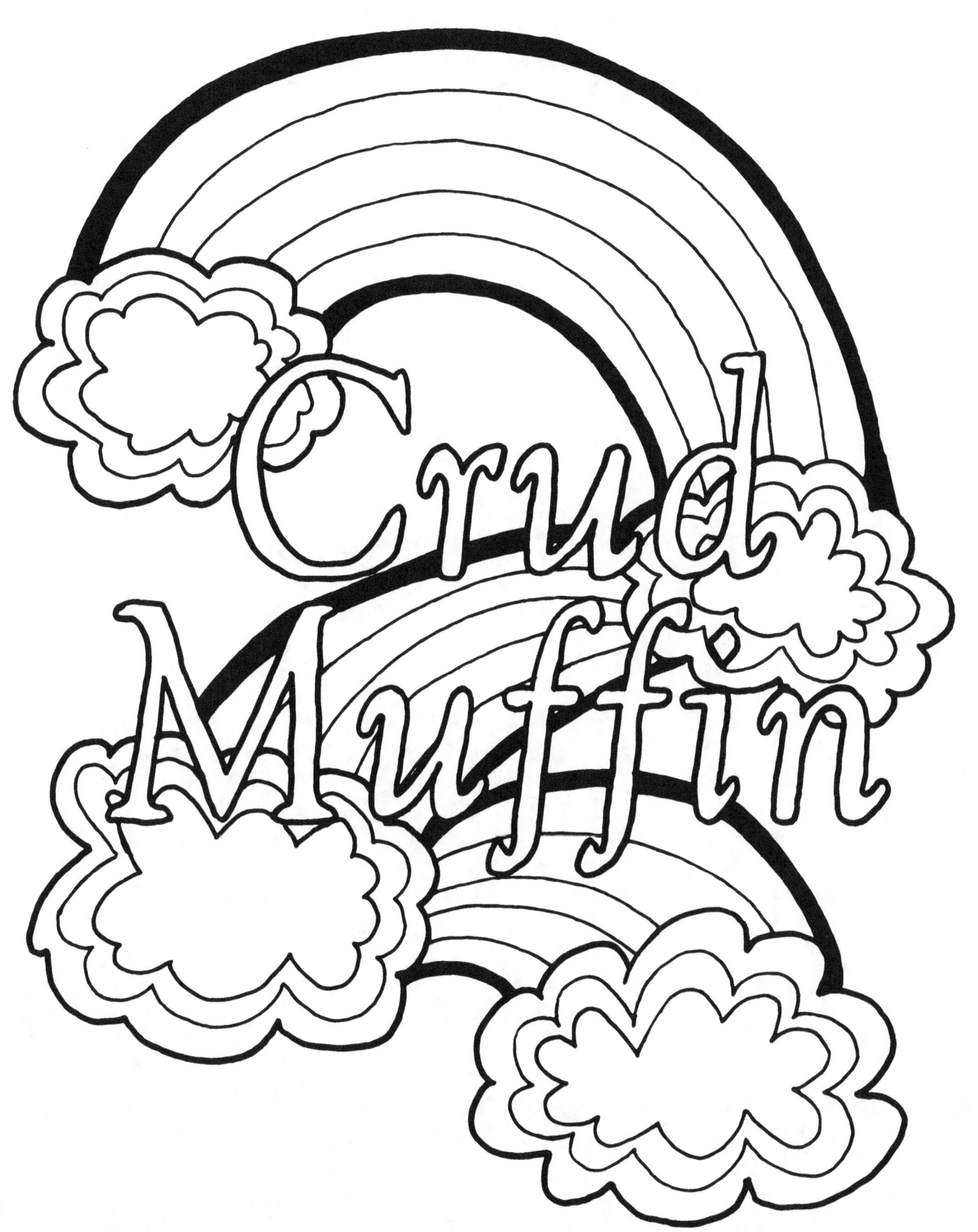

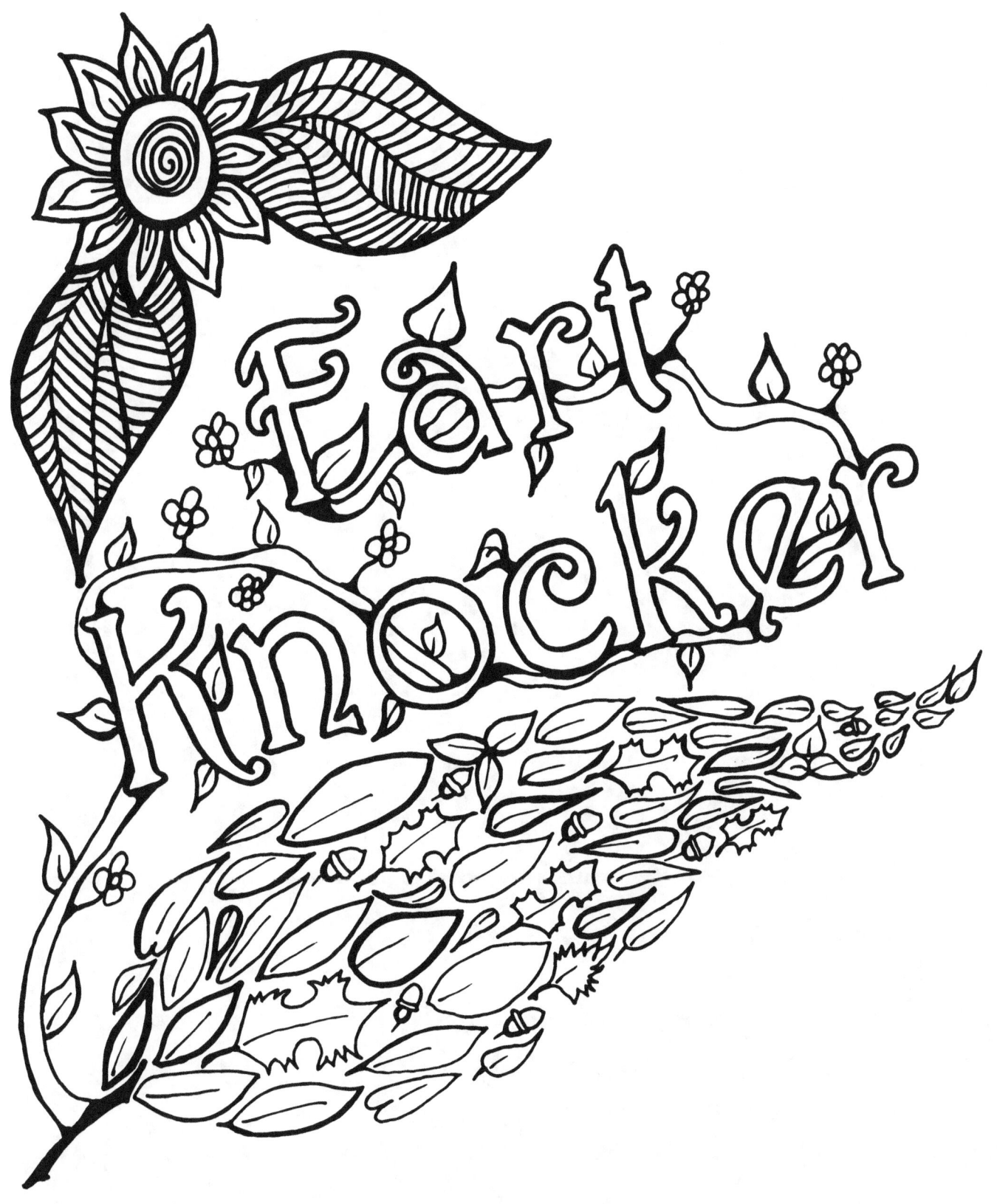

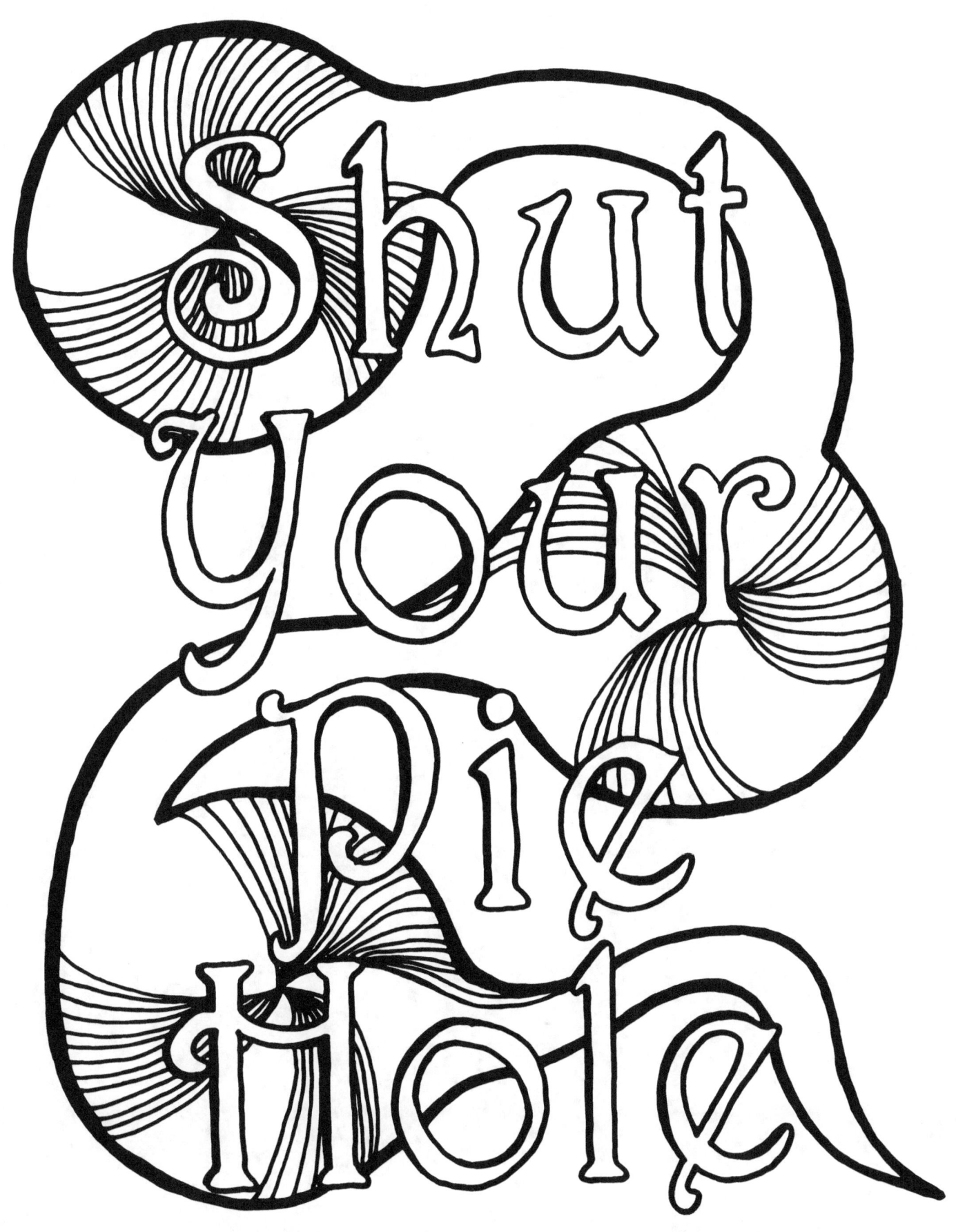

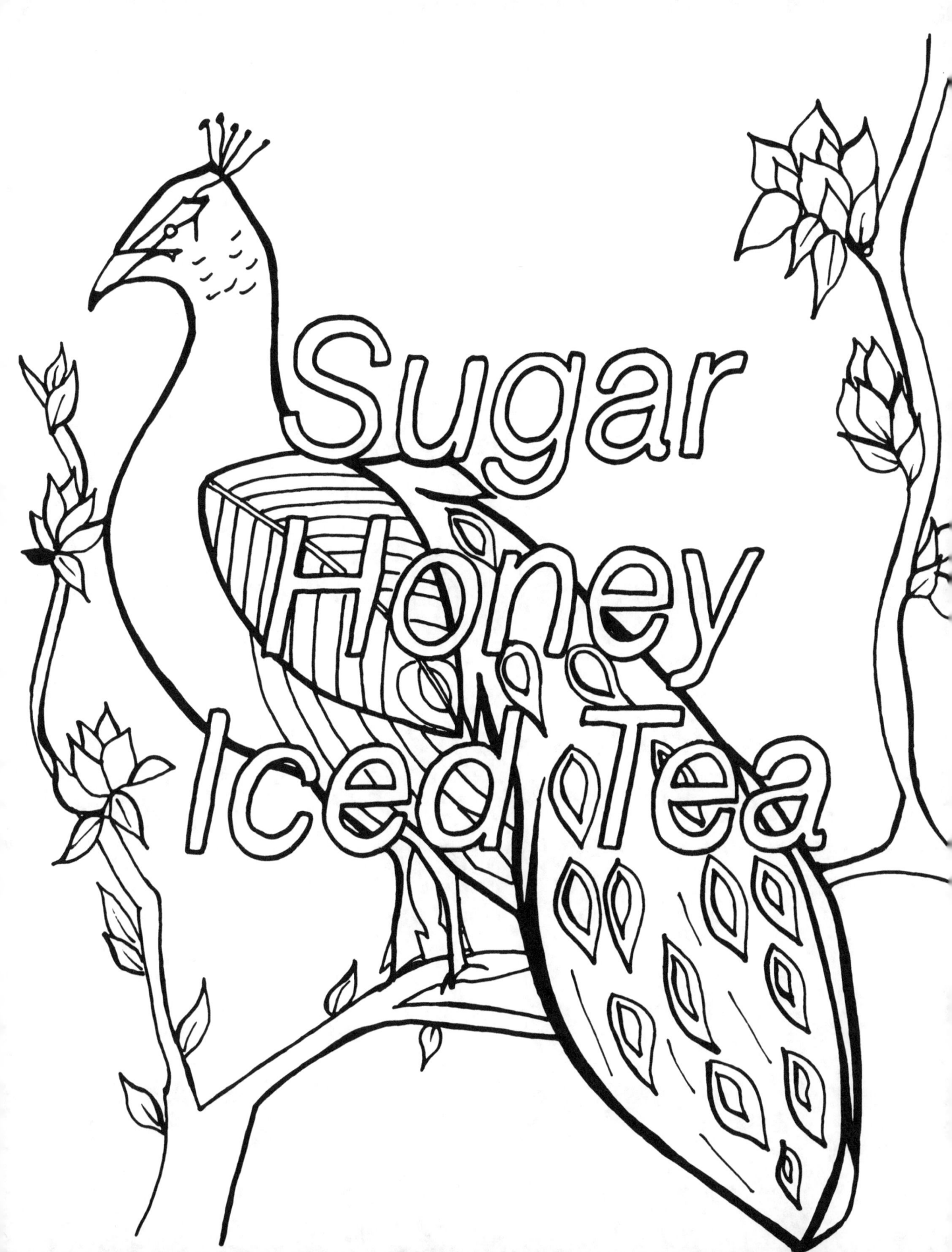

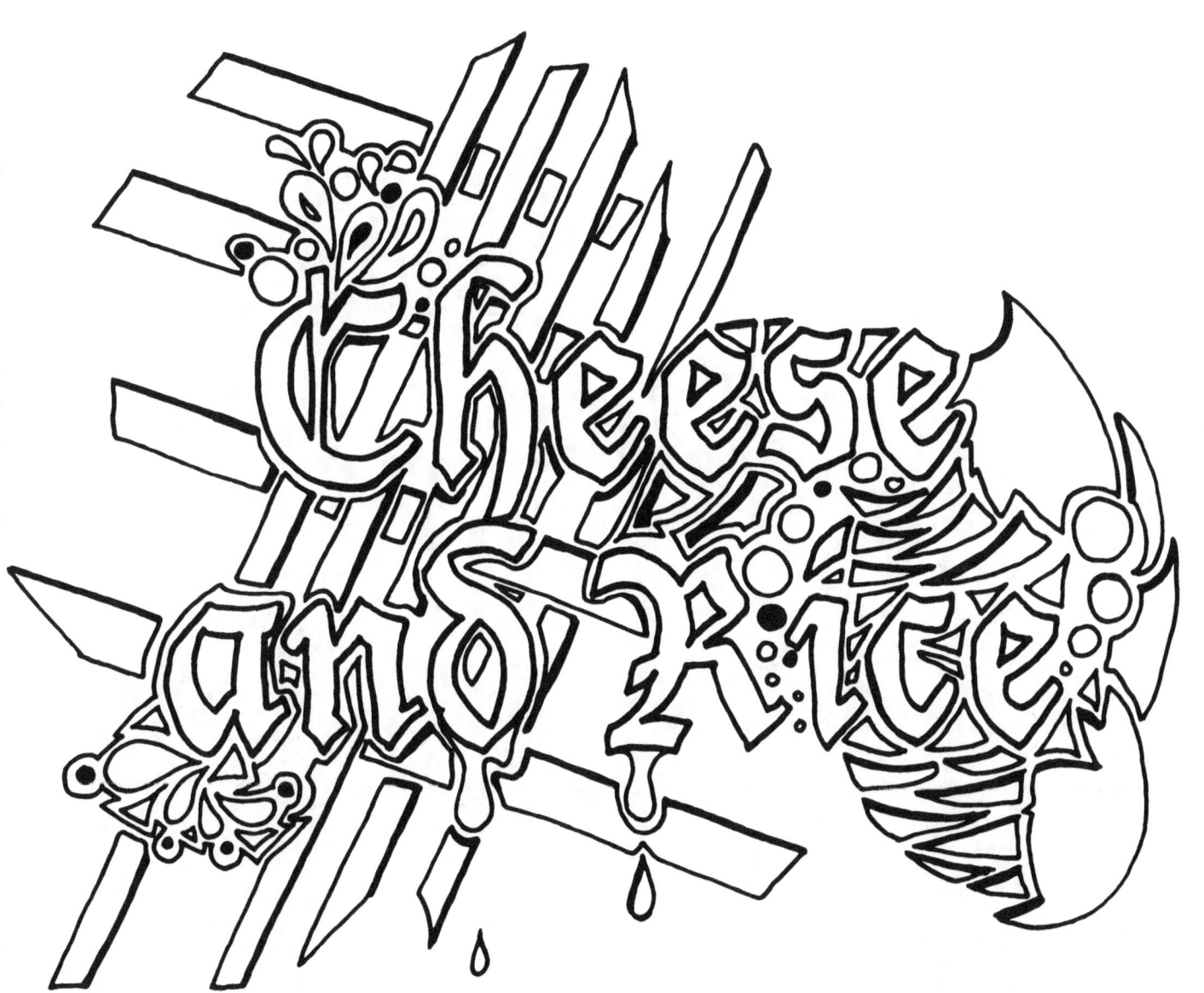

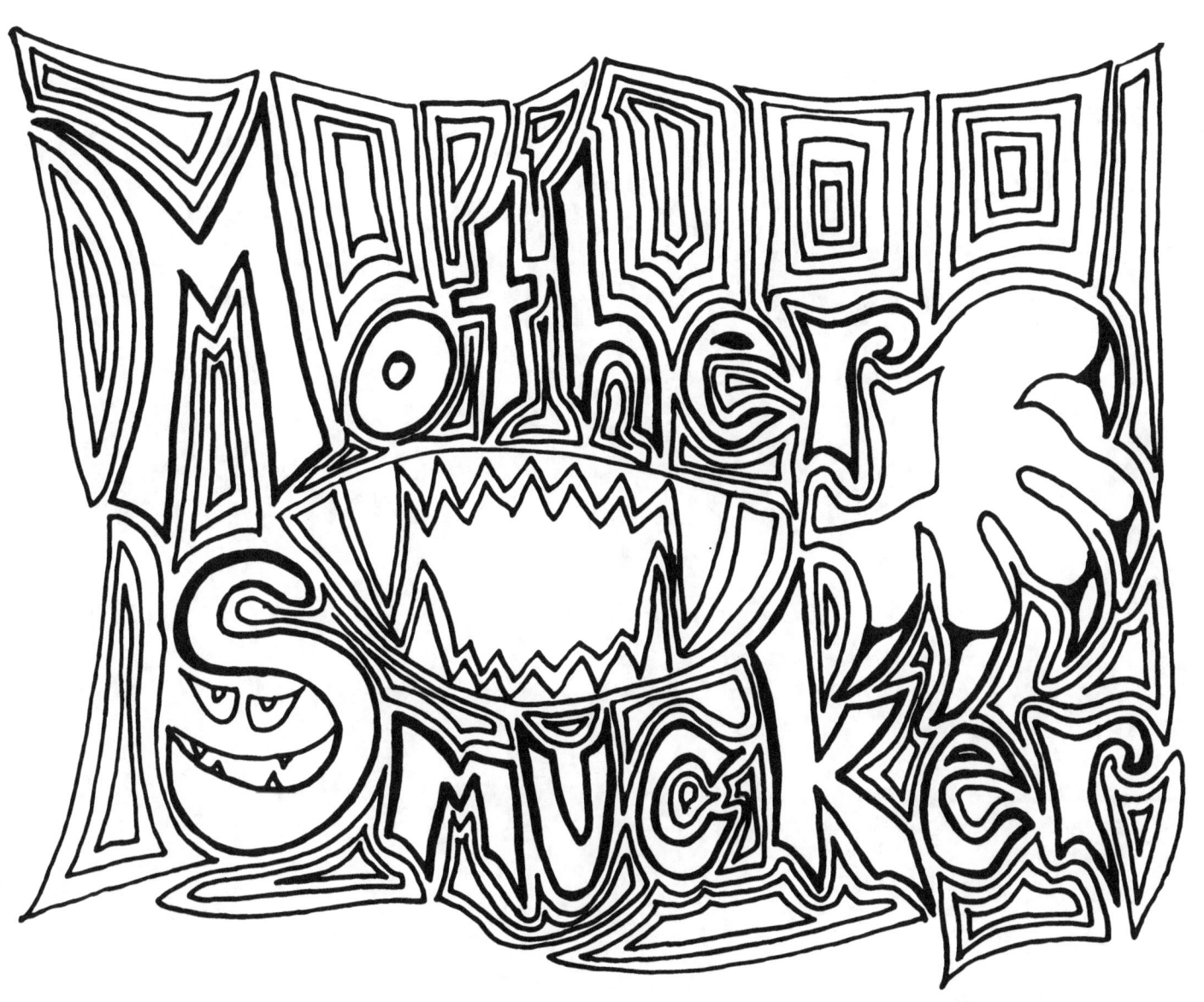

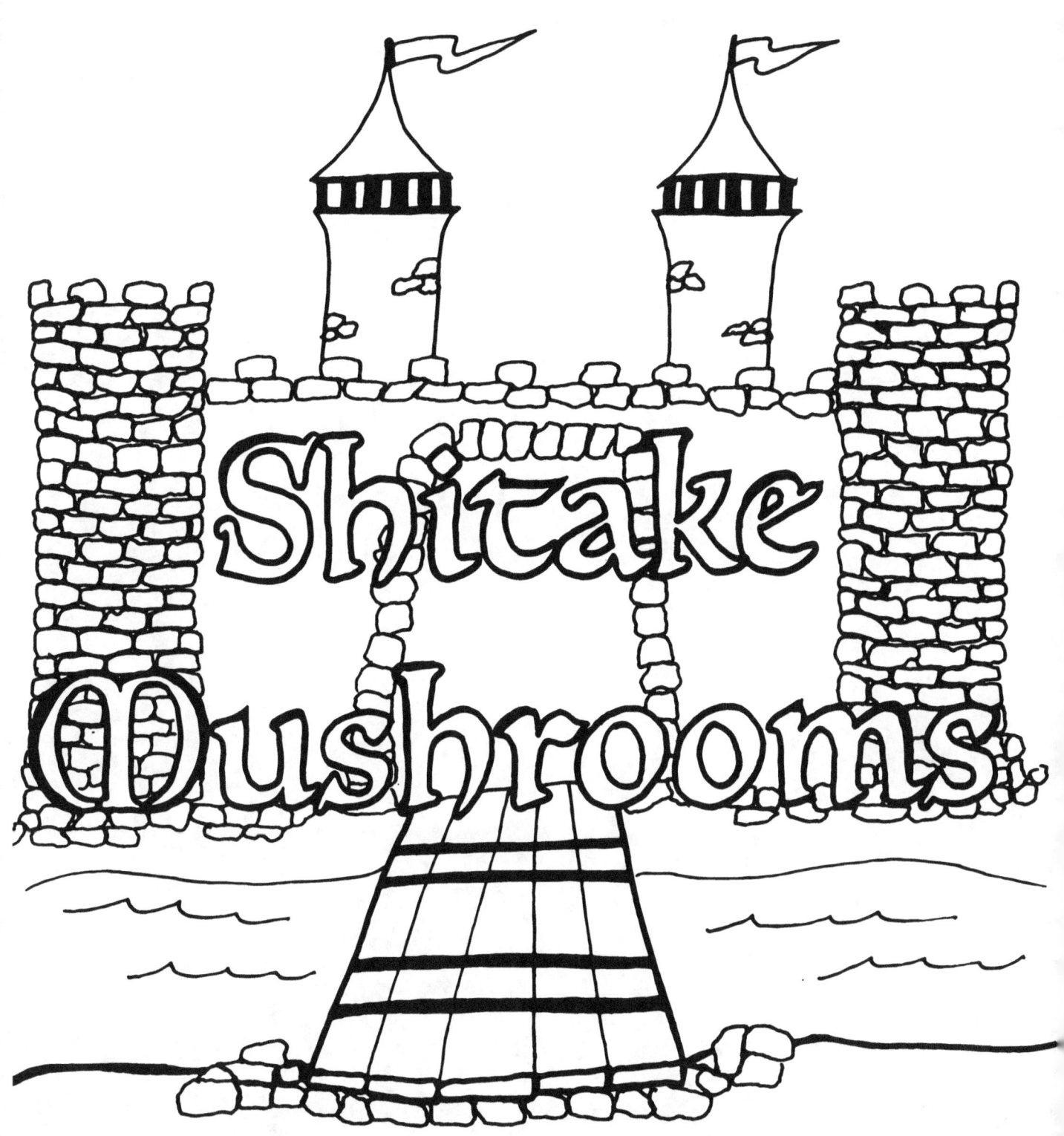

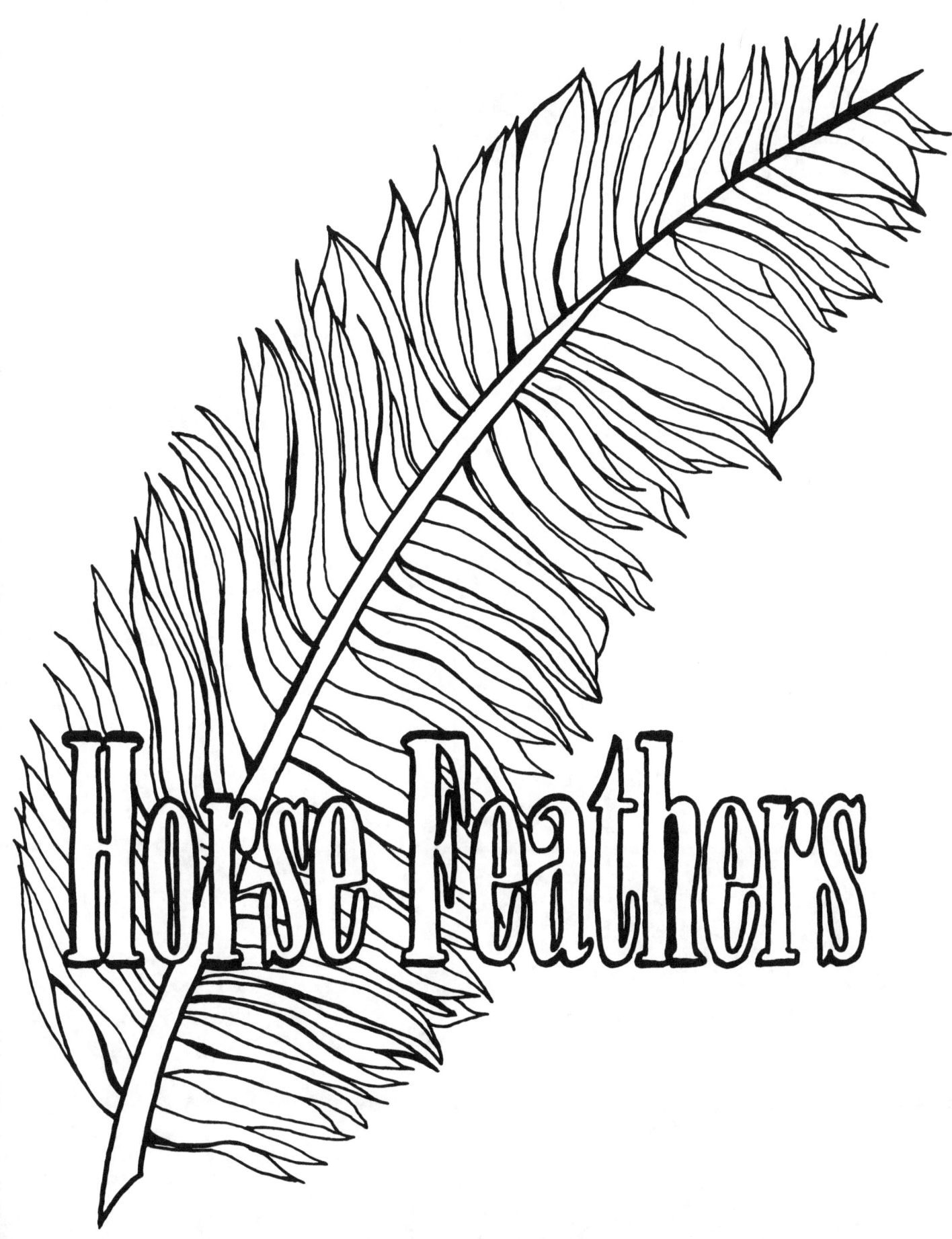

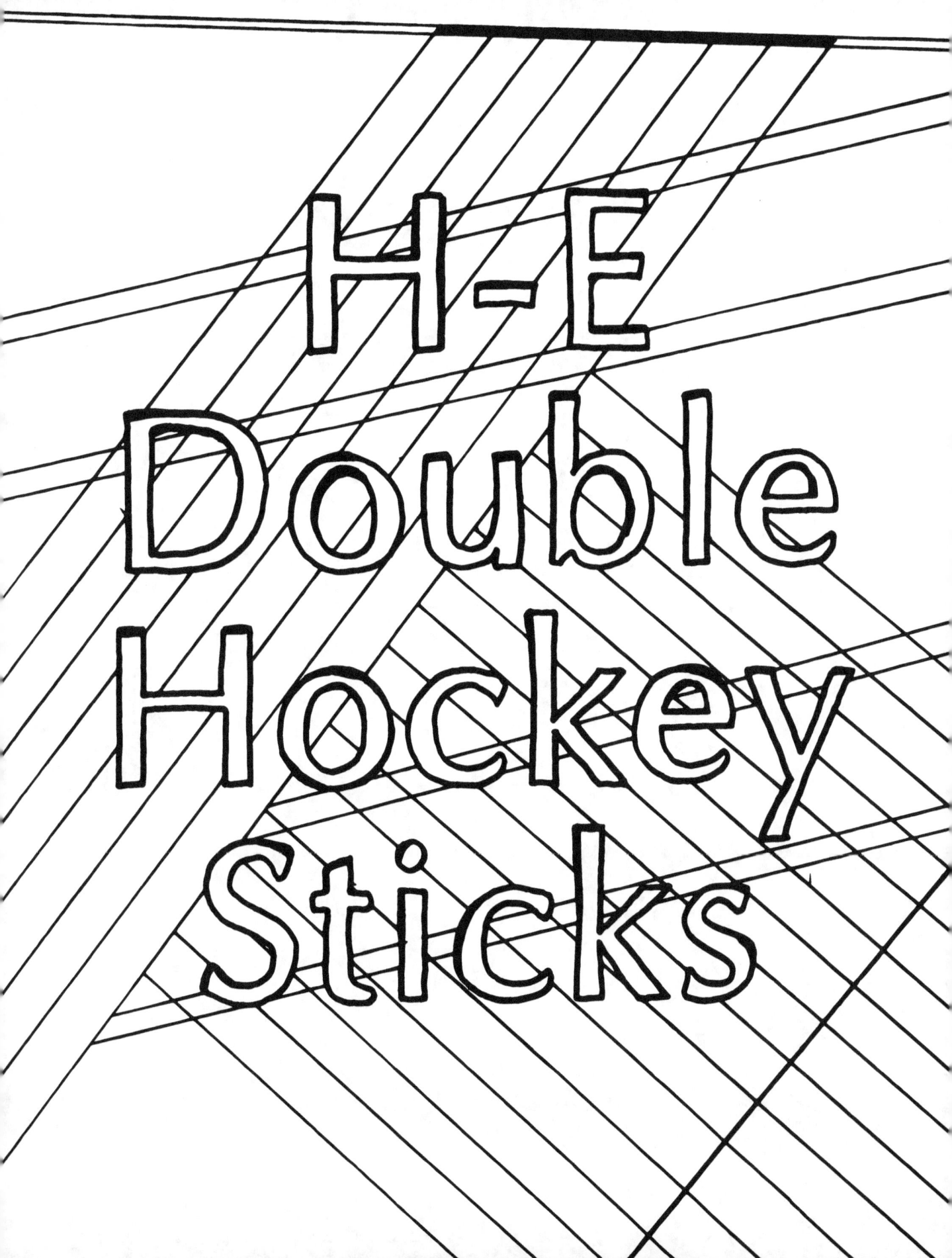

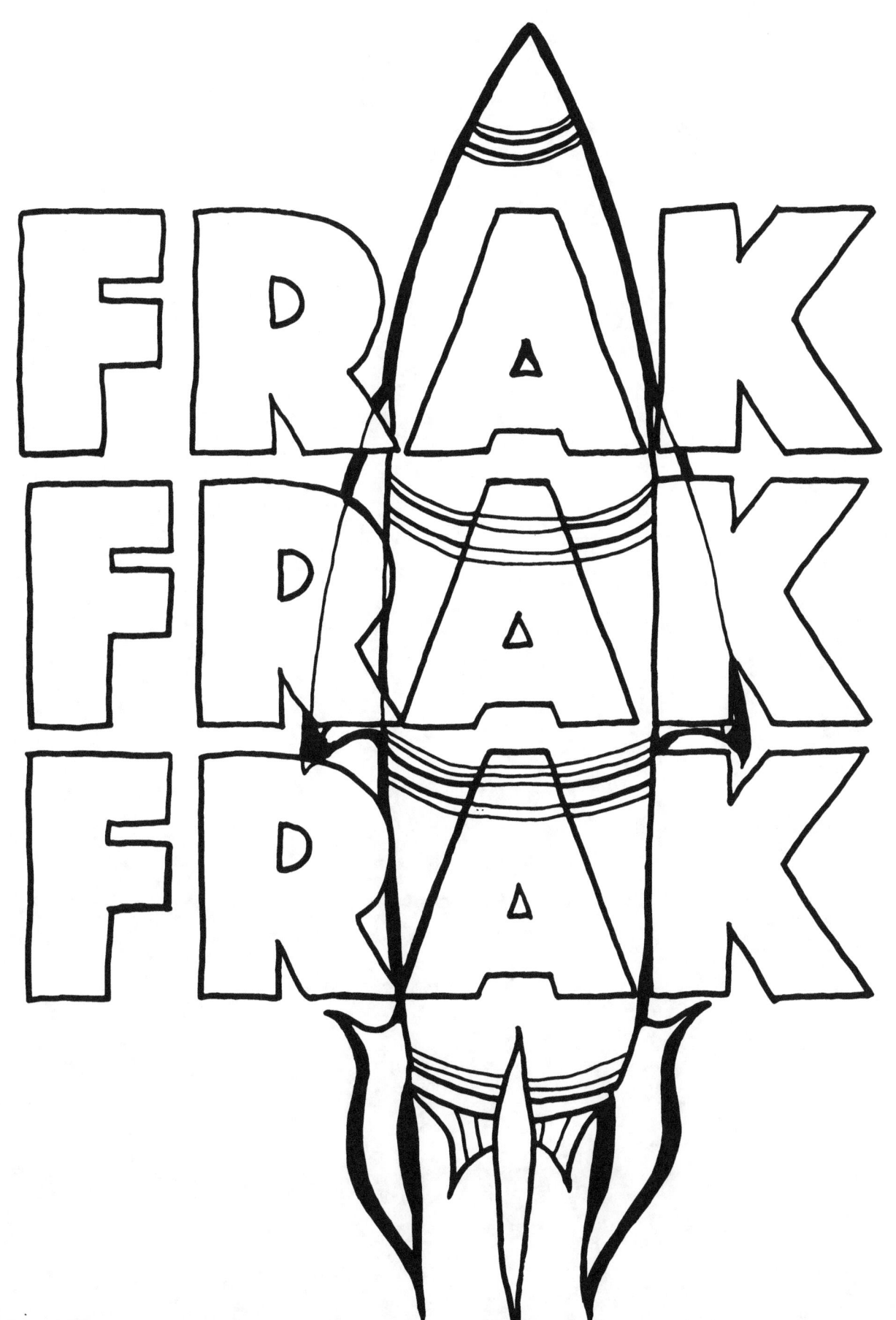

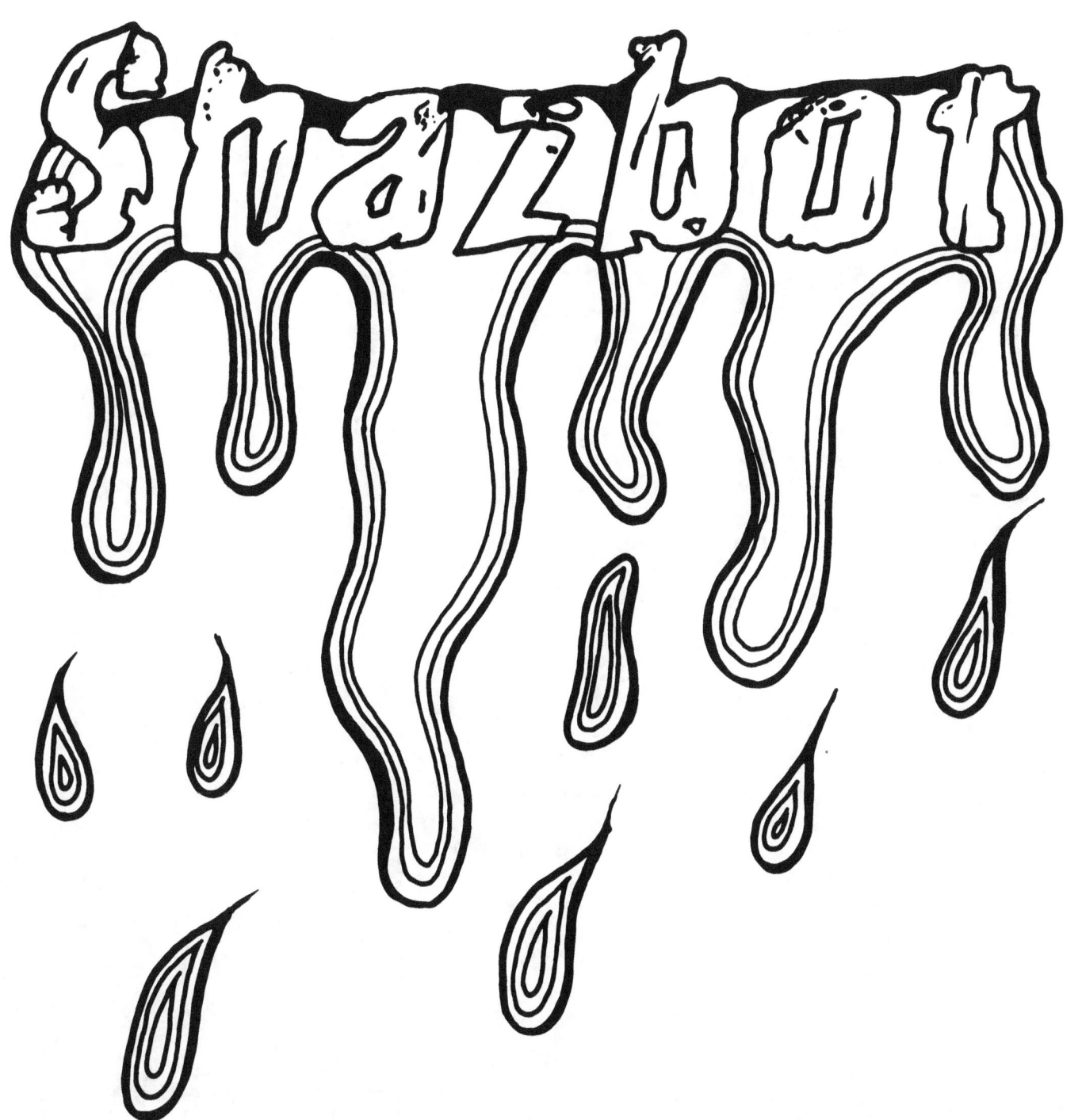

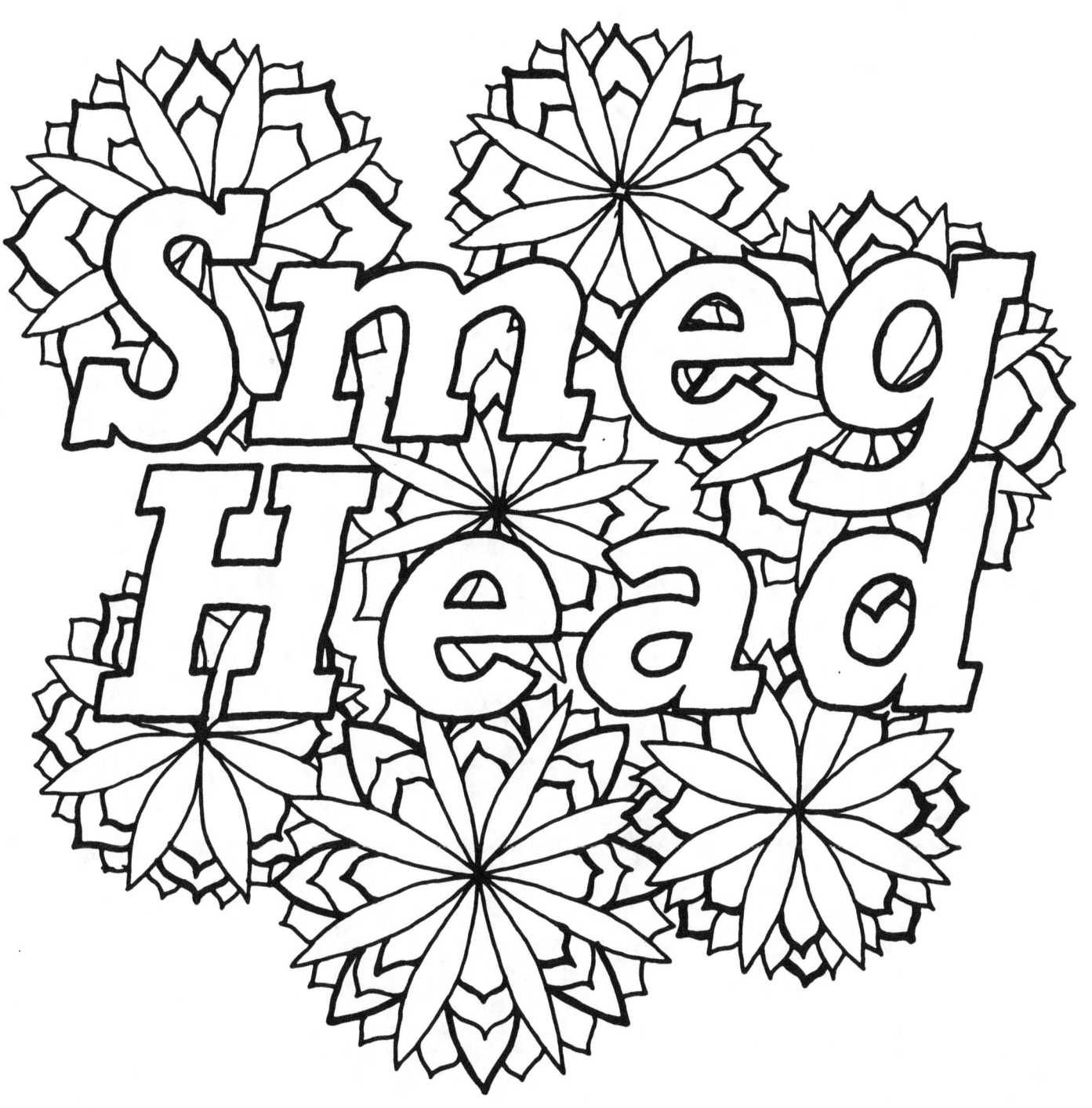

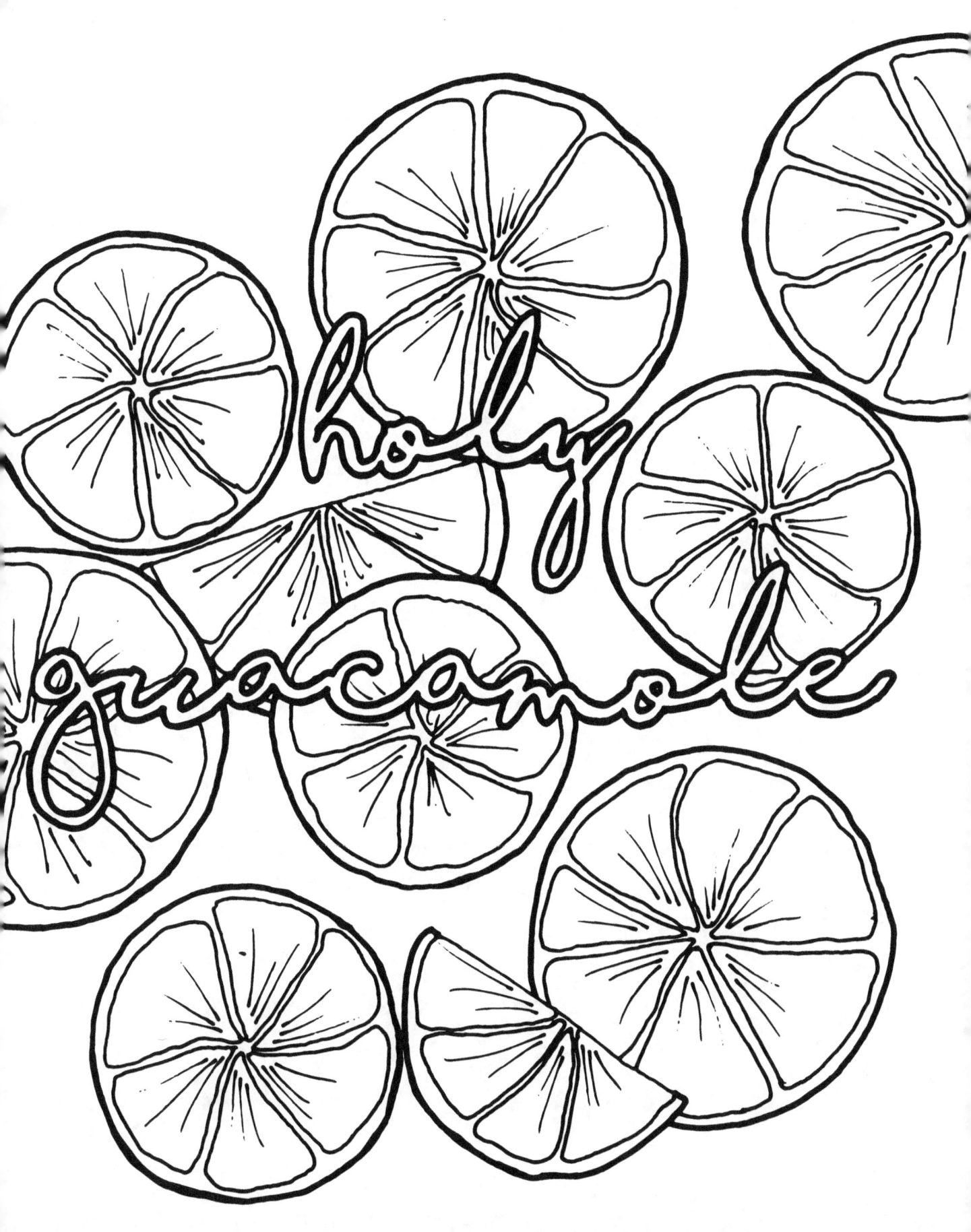

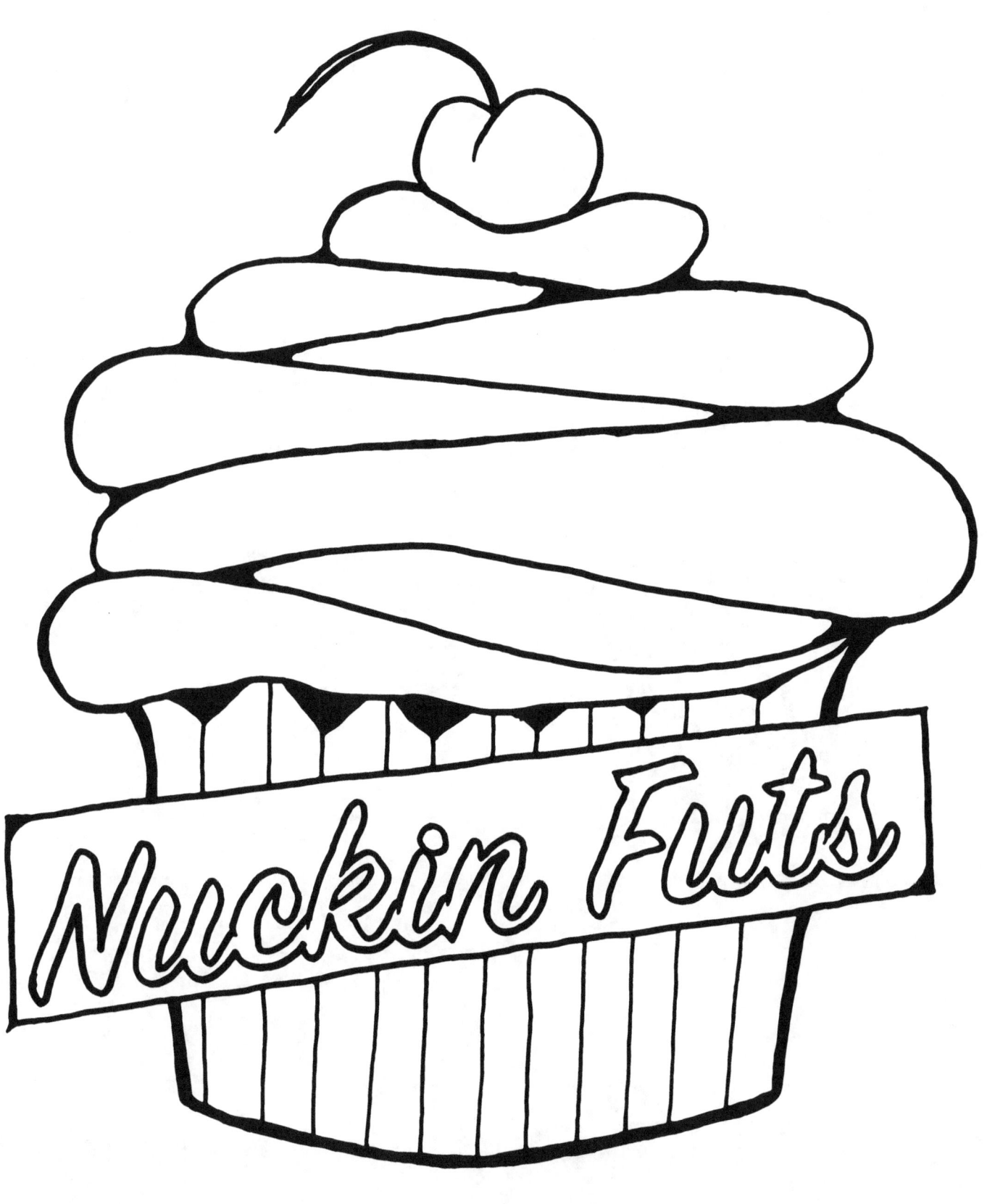

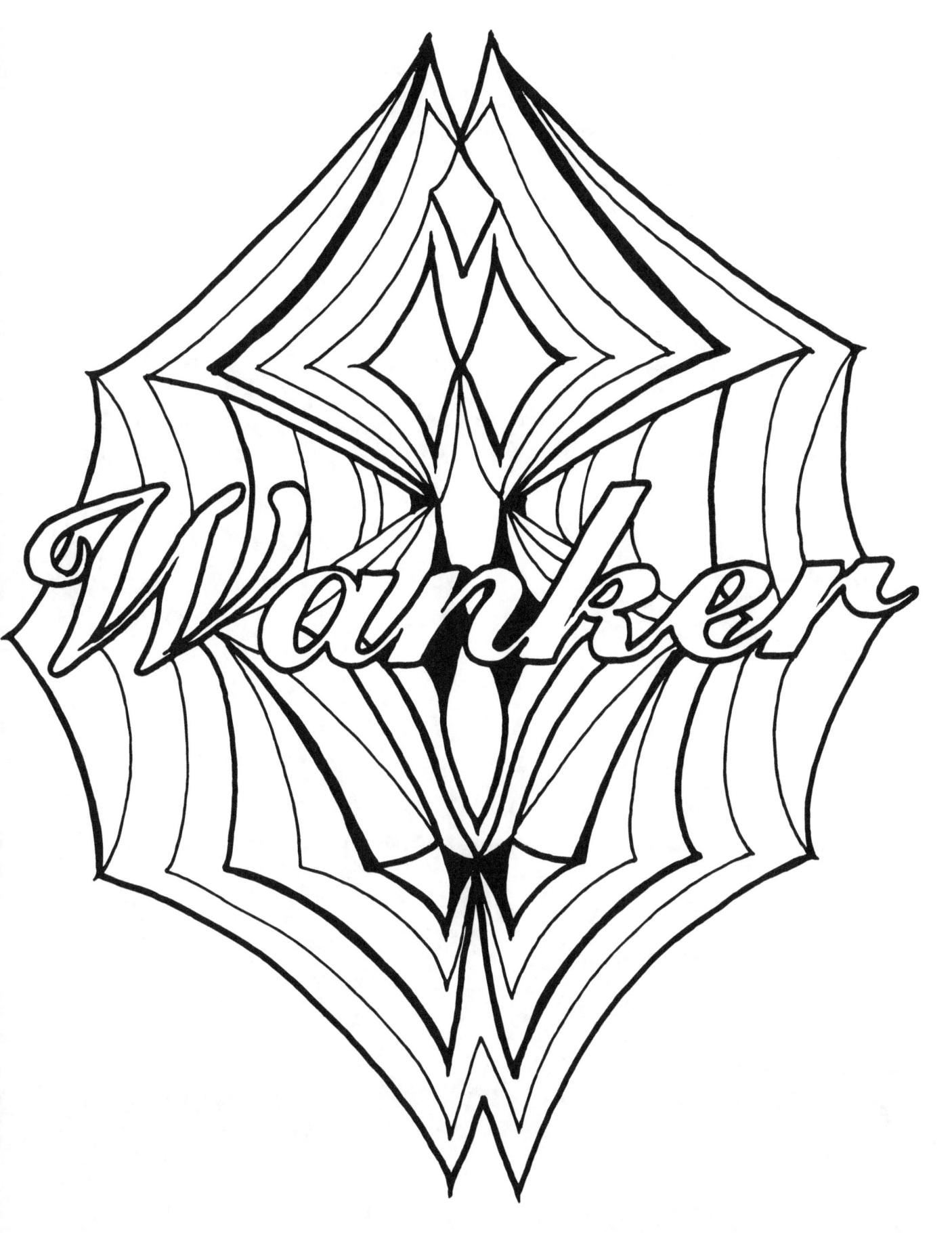

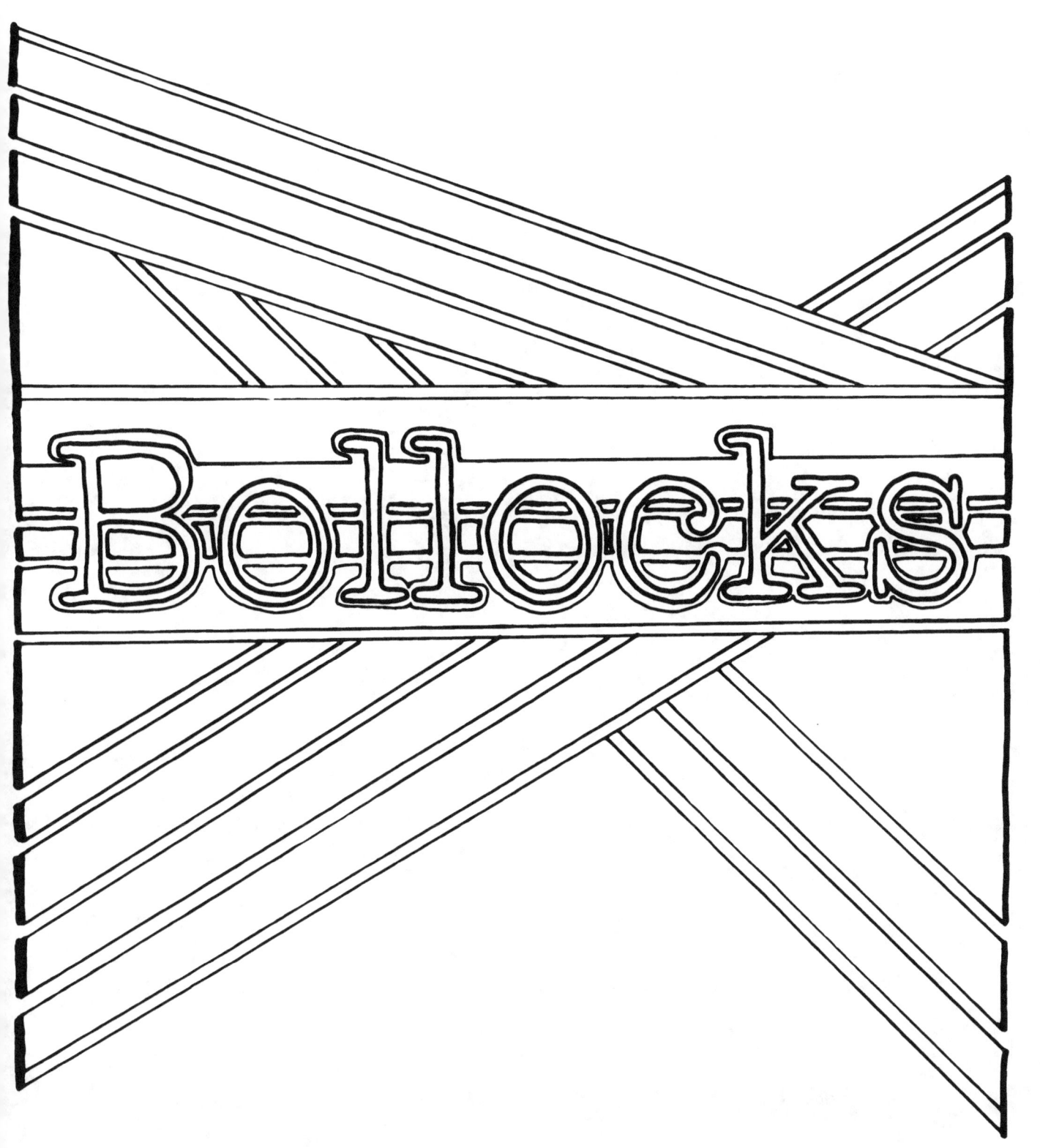

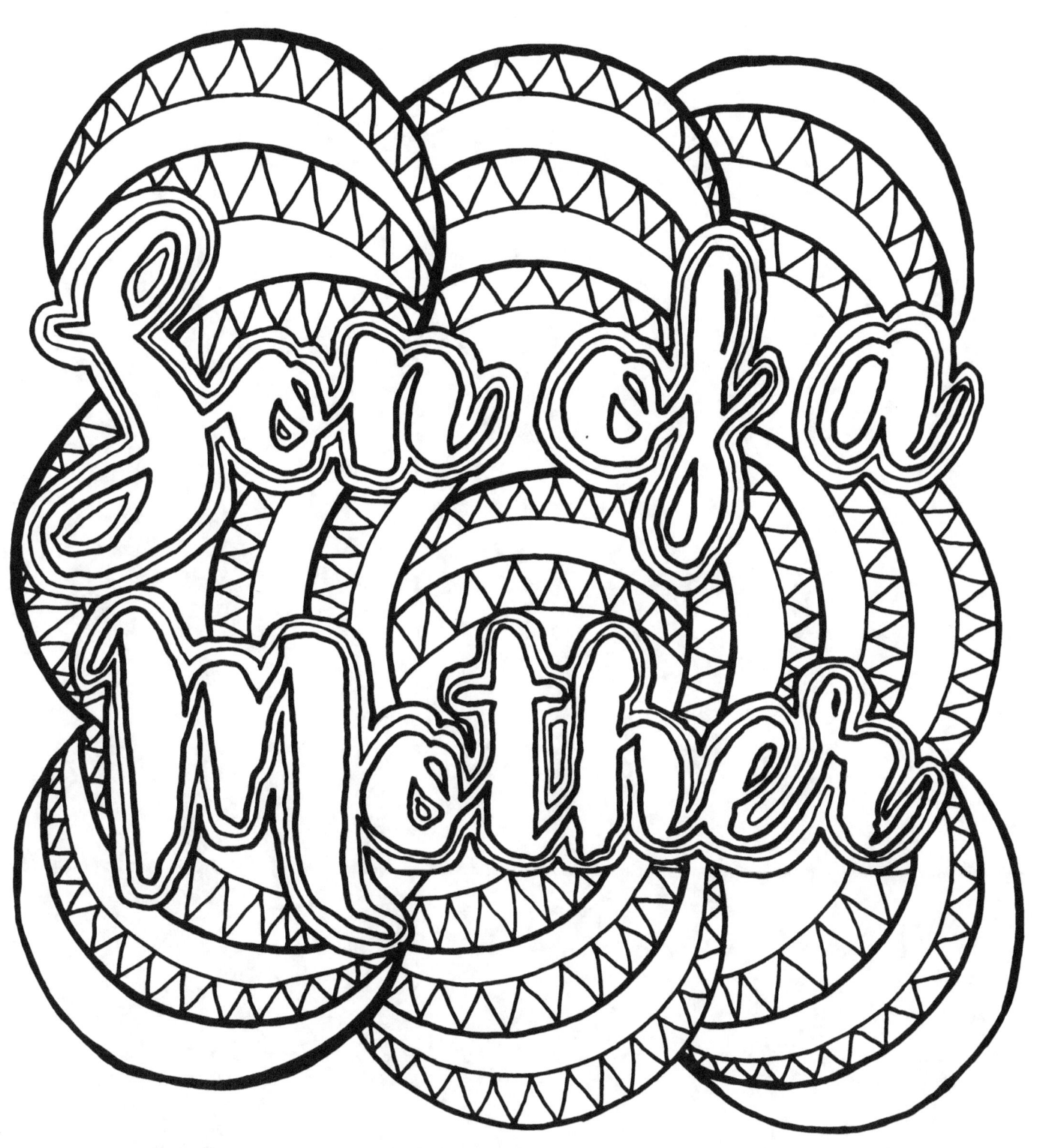

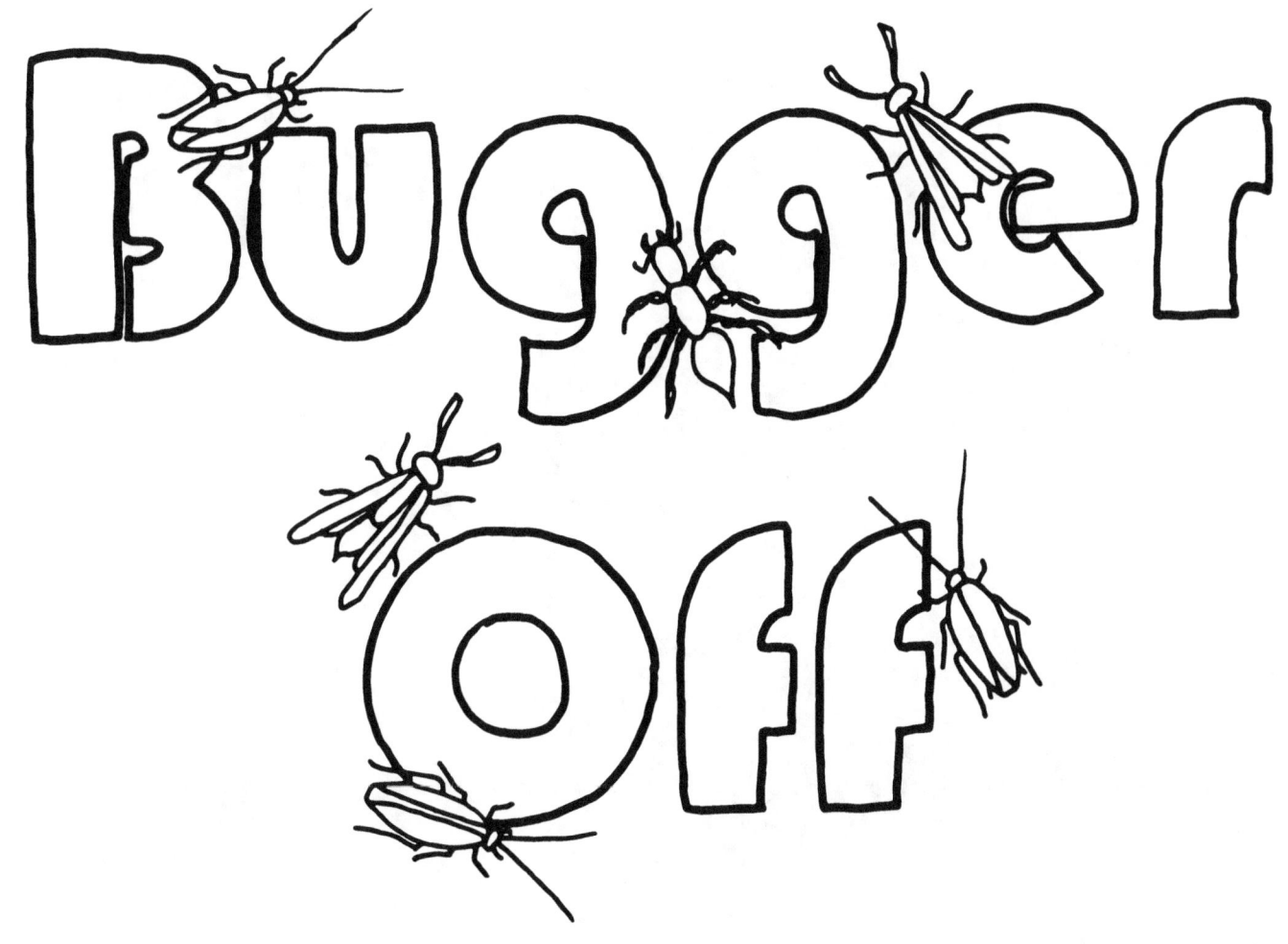

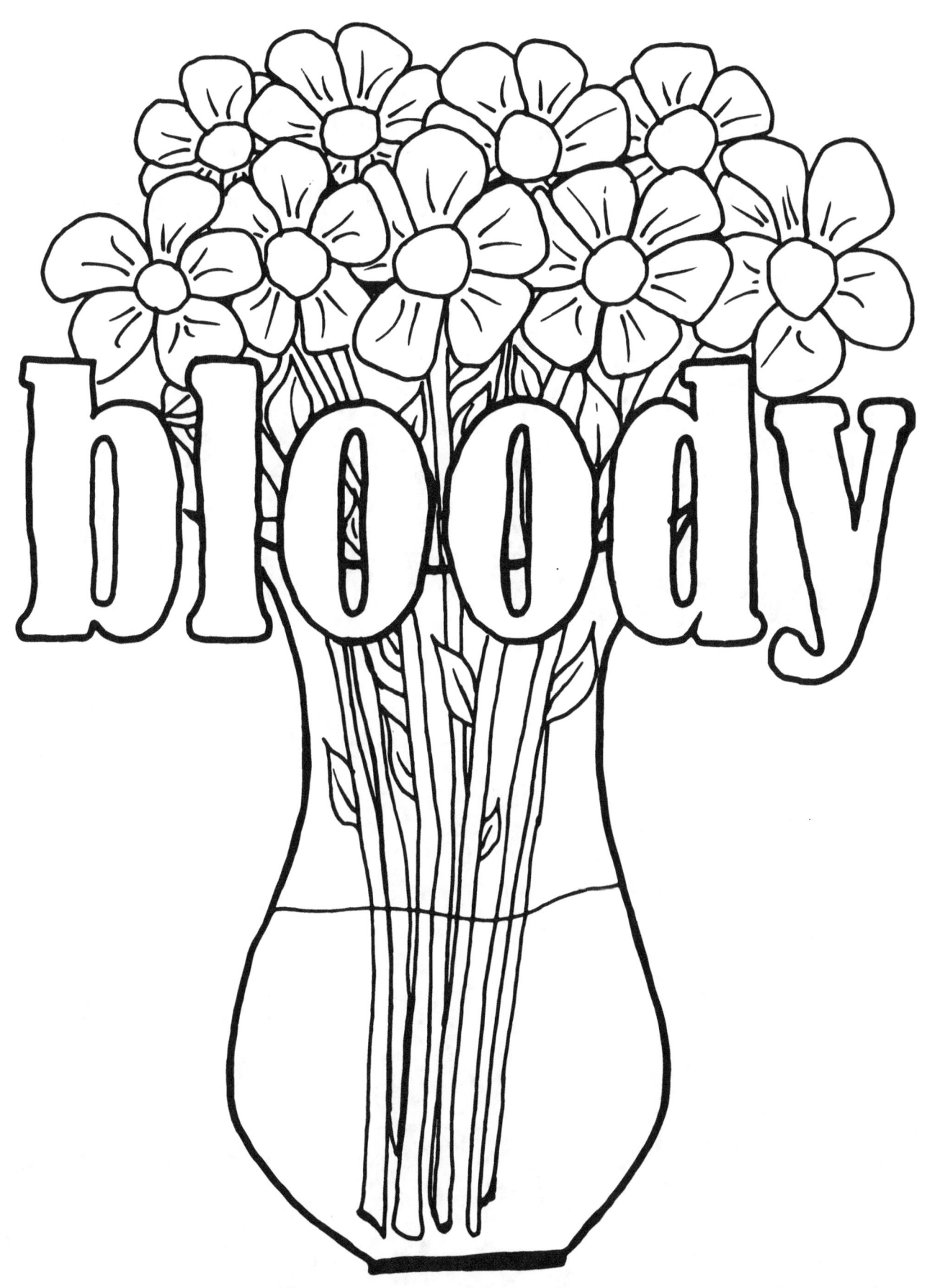

Bonus pages from other Coloring for Life coloring books

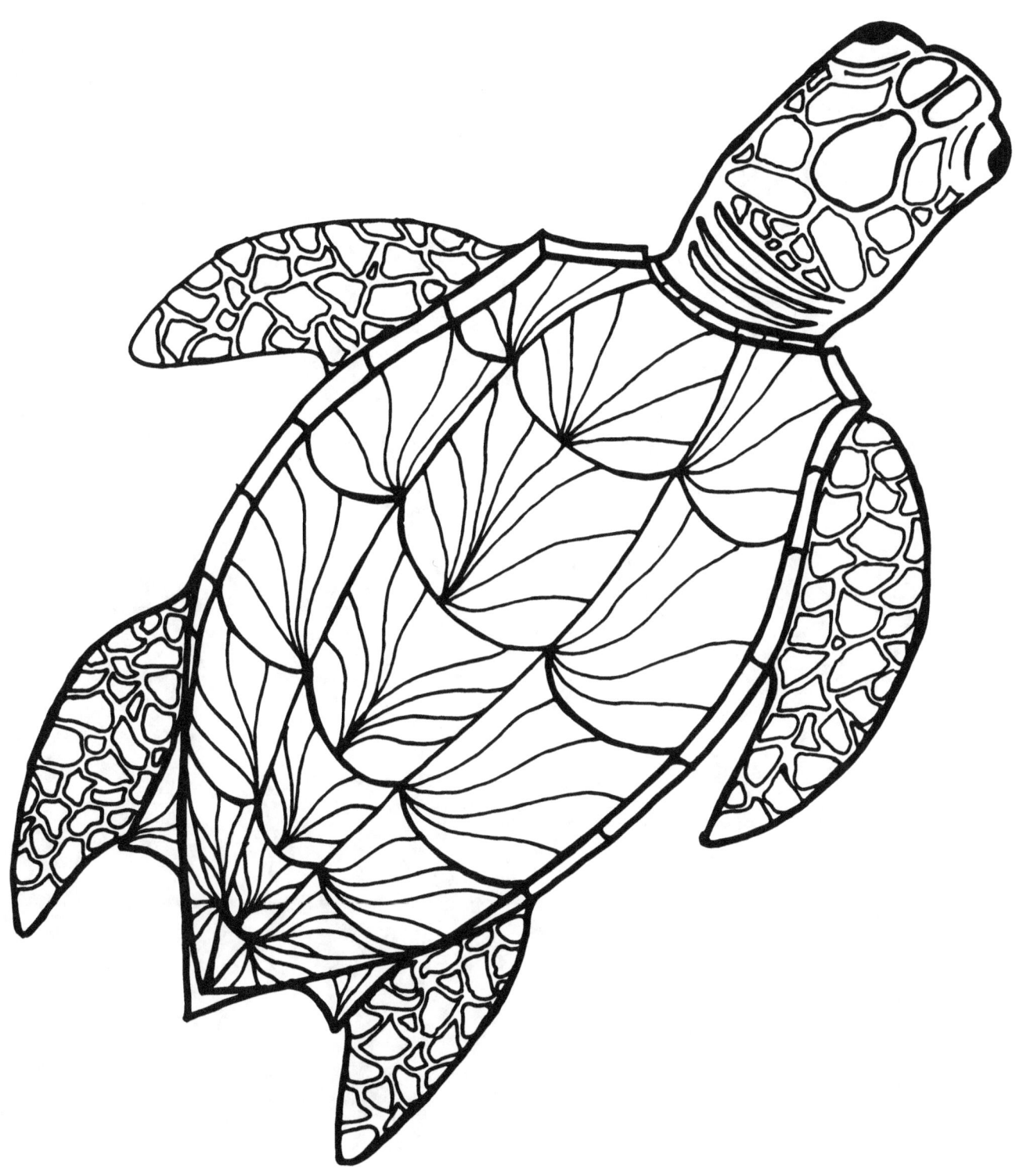

From the book "Colorful Coast" by Bill Clanton

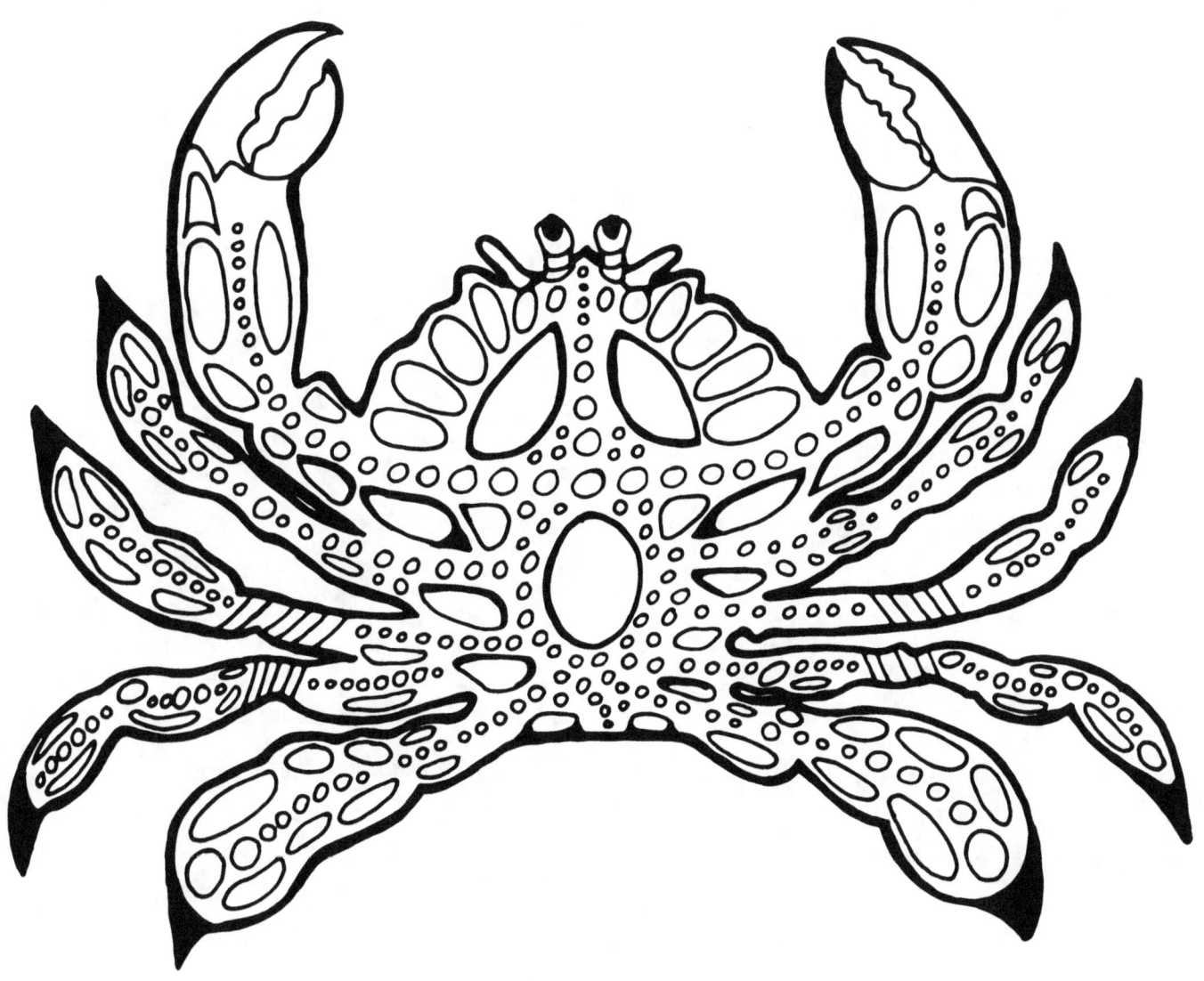

From the book "Colorful Coast" by Bill Clanton

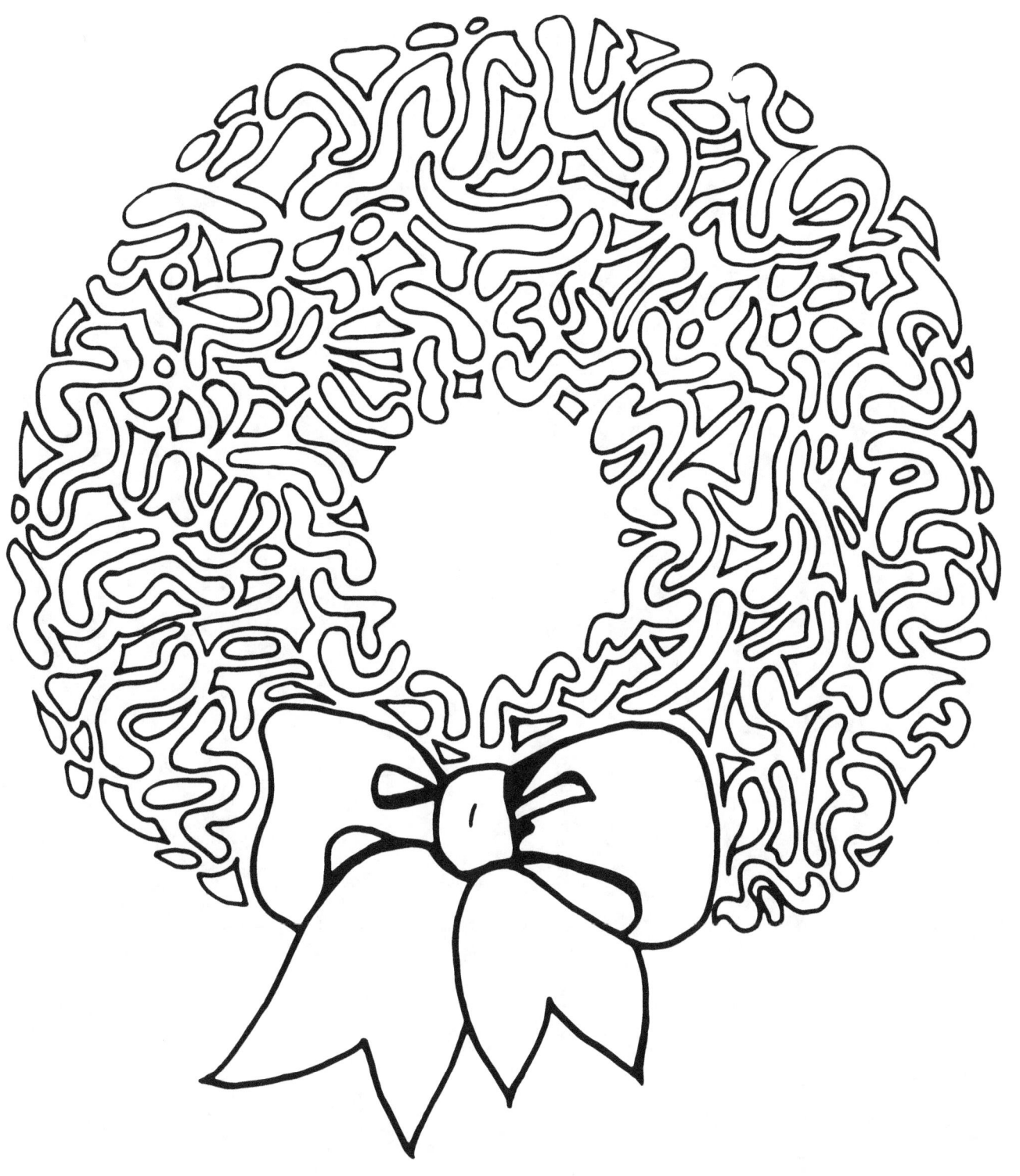

From the book "Colorful Christmas" by Bill Clanton

If you enjoyed this book, please look for other Coloring for Life coloring books.

Coloring for Life: Colorful Quotes
- ISBN-13: 978-0-9974996-0-5

Coloring for Life: Colorful Christmas
- ISBN-13: 978-0-9974996-1-2

Coloring for Life: Colorful Coast
- ISBN-13: 978-0-9974996-2-9

Coloring for Life: Colorful Coast (Long Beach Island Edition)
- ISBN-13: 978-0-9974996-3-6

Coloring for Life: Colorful Coast (Cape May, NJ Edition)
- ISBN-13: 978-0-9974996-4-3

If you've ever considered making your own coloring book for grown ups, look for Bill Clanton's guide outlining the steps necessary to get your book published.

Creating a Coloring Book for Adults: Learn the Secrets to Getting Your Coloring Book Published

Kindle:
ASIN: B0194D3GI6

Paperback:
- ISBN-10: 1519761872
- ISBN-13: 978-1519761873

www.ingramcontent.com/pod-product-compliance
Lightning Source LLC
Chambersburg PA
CBHW080841170526
45158CB00009B/2604